THE POET
CHILDREN
Duck

ANTHOLOGY

PUFFIN BOOKS

DUCKS AND DRAGONS

'Children take to poetry like ducks to water,' says Gene Kemp in her introduction, and this has certainly been her own experience in the classroom. All the poems in *Ducks and Dragons* have been read with children and enjoyed by them, sometimes in class, sometimes individually and in odd moments.

They range in date from Chaucer to contemporaries, and in mood from the boisterous to the melancholy. They are divided into eight sections which include Seasons, Animals and Friends, and A Finger of Fear – but there is great variety and tone in each section.

This is a satisfying and approachable anthology which contains something for all moods and temperaments.

Gene Kemp was born in a small Midlands village, the youngest of a large family. She took a degree in English at Exeter University. She has three children and a politically motivated husband, with whom she is heavily involved in local politics.

Ducks and Dragons

Poems for Children

edited by Gene Kemp

Illustrated by Carolyn Dinan

Puffin Books
in association with
Faber & Faber

PUFFIN BOOKS

Penguin Books Ltd, 27 Wrights Lane, London w8 5TZ (Publishing and Editorial)
and Harmondsworth, Middlesex, England (Distribution and Warehouse)
Viking Penguin Inc., 40 West 23rd Street, New York, New York 10010, USA
Penguin Books Australia Ltd, Ringwood, Victoria, Australia
Penguin Books Canada Ltd, 2801 John Street, Markham, Ontario, Canada L3R 1B4
Penguin Books (NZ) Ltd, 182–190 Wairau Road, Auckland 10, New Zealand

First published by Faber & Faber Ltd 1980
Published in Puffin Books 1983
Reprinted 1986, 1988

This collection copyright © Gene Kemp, 1980
Illustrations copyright © Faber & Faber Ltd, 1980
All rights reserved

Printed and bound in Great Britain by
Cox & Wyman Ltd, Reading
Set in Bembo

For Phyllis

Contents

A FINGER OF FEAR

OLD SONGS TO SING: OLD TALES TO TELL

AND EVENING ENDS

Acknowledgements

The editor is grateful for permission to use the following copyright material:

"Days" from *The Whitsun Weddings* by Philip Larkin. Reprinted by permission of Faber & Faber Ltd.

"The Fight of the Year" from *Watchwords* copyright © 1969 by Roger McGough.

"April Birthday" from *Season Songs* and "My Brother Bert" from *Meet My Folks* by Ted Hughes. Reprinted by permission of Faber & Faber Ltd.

"Mr. Bidery's Spidery Garden" from *Mr. Bidery's Spidery Garden* by David McCord, by permission of George G. Harrap & Co. Ltd., and Little Brown & Company. Copyright © 1970 by David McCord.

"Autumn" from *The Little White Gate* by Florence Hoatson, published by George G. Harrap & Company Ltd.

"Sweet Chestnuts" from *The Roundabout by the Sea* by John Walsh, by permission of Mrs. A. M. Walsh.

"Chips" from *Come Along: Poems for Younger Children* by Stanley Cook, published by Stanley Cook, The Polytechnic, Huddersfield.

"If You Don't Put Your Shoes On" from *Mind Your Own Business* by Michael Rosen, published by André Deutsch Ltd. Second edition 1978.

"Child on Top of a Greenhouse" and "The Serpent" by Theodore Roethke. Reprinted by permission of Faber & Faber Ltd. from *The Collected Poems of Theodore Roethke*. "Child on

14

Lines from "The Song of Quoodle" from *The Flying Inn* by G. K. Chesterton, by permission of the Estate of the late G. K. Chesterton.

"Jim-Jam Pyjamas" by Gina Wilson, by permission of the author.

"The Family" from *Widdy-Widdy-Wurkey* by Rose Fyleman, published by Basil Blackwell.

"The Marrog" by R. C. Scriven, by permission of the author.

"Fairy Story" from *The Collected Poems of Stevie Smith*, published by Allen Lane, by permission of James MacGibbon as the author's executor.

"What Has Happened to Lulu?" from *Collected Poems* by Charles Causley, published by Macmillan.

"Hide and Seek" from *Walking Wounded* by Vernon Scannell, published by Eyre & Spottiswoode Ltd., by permission of the author.

"The Wind was on the Withered Heath" from *The Hobbit* by J. R. R. Tolkien, published by George Allen & Unwin (Publishers) Ltd.

"Steam Shovel" from *From Upper Pasture* by Charles Malam. Copyright 1930, © 1958 by Charles Malam. Reprinted by permission of Holt, Rinehart and Winston, Publishers.

"A Small Dragon" from *Notes to the Hurrying Man* by Brian Patten, published by George Allen & Unwin (Publishers) Ltd.

"Spinning Song" from *Collected Poems* by Edith Sitwell, published by Macmillan.

"A Smugglers' Song" from *Rewards and Fairies* by Rudyard Kipling, by permission of the National Trust and Macmillan London Ltd.

"Aedh Wishes for the Cloths of Heaven" from *Collected Poems* by W. B. Yeats, by permission of M. B. Yeats and Macmillan London Ltd.

Introduction

———◆———

Children take to poetry like ducks to water.
　No little child can resist
　　　　　"One, two, three, four, five,
　　　　　Once I caught a fish alive,"
or
　　　　　"This little piggy went to market."
　This love need not be lost later. The rhythms, colours, shapes,
sounds, the jollity, the excitement, the images, the sadness, the
changing moods and scenes can weave a spell for footballers as
well as dreamers. There is something for all, a James Reeves or
a Michael Rosen, an elegy or a limerick, a ballad or a play-
ground jingle. And

　　　　　"There's comfort for the comfortless,
　　　　　There's honey for the bee. . . ."

　I've tried to make a mixture of poems in this collection. Some
are familiar. Some not. All have been read with children, often
at odd moments, in little spaces in the day, just right for fitting
a poem into, and like the moments themselves some are for
greater thoughts and ideas, some just for little ones, and some
just for a . . . giggle or two. Children love words, words, words
—riddles and jokes and tongue-twisters—and they love poems
too. In the poetry books they keep, they mix their own poems
with the ones they copy.
　"Shall I make my writing today a story or a poem?" they ask.

"Whichever *you* like," I say.
And,
"Which poem shall I write out in my book?"
"Whichever *you* like," I say.

Gene Kemp

Beginning . . .

The World is Day-breaking

The world is day-breaking!
The world is day-breaking!

Day arises
From its sleep.
Day wakes up
With the dawning light.

The world is day-breaking!
The world is day-breaking!

ANON.

(Papuan dawn song and Eskimo song)

Days

What are days for?
Days are where we live.
They come, they wake us
Time and time over.
They are to be happy in:
Where can we live but days . . . ?

PHILIP LARKIN
from *Days*

Time to Get Up

A birdie with a yellow bill
Hopped upon the window sill,
Cocked his shining eye and said:
"Aint you 'shamed, you sleepy-head?"

ROBERT LOUIS STEVENSON

Seasons

The Fight of the Year

"And there goes the bell for the third month
and Winter comes out of its corner looking groggy
Spring leads with a left to the head
followed by a sharp right to the body
    daffodils
    primroses
    crocuses
    snowdrops
    lilacs
    violets
    pussywillow
Winter can't take much more punishment
and Spring shows no signs of tiring
    tadpoles
    squirrels
    baalambs
    badgers
    bunny rabbits
    mad march hares
    horses and hounds
Spring is merciless
Winter won't go the full twelve rounds
    bobtail clouds
    scallywaggy winds
    the sun
    a pavement artist
    in every town
A left to the chin
and Winter's down!
    1 tomatoes

2 radish
3 cucumber
4 onions
5 beetroot
6 celery
7 and any
8 amount
9 of lettuce
10 for dinner
Winter's out for the count
Spring is the winner!"

ROGER MCGOUGH

Spring Song

The year's at the spring
And day's at the morn;
Morning's at seven;
The hillside's dew-pearled;
The lark's on the wing;
The snail's on the thorn;
God's in his heaven—
All's right with the world!

ROBERT BROWNING
from Pippa Passes

April Birthday

When your birthday brings the world under your window
  And the song-thrush sings wet-throated in the dew
And aconite and primrose are unsticking the wrappers
  Of the package that has come today for you

    Lambs bounce out and stand astonished
    Puss willow pushes among bare branches
    Sooty hawthorns shiver into emerald

                    And a new air
    Nuzzles the sugary
    Buds of the chestnut. A groundswell and a stir
    Billows the silvered
    Violet silks
    Of the south—a tenderness
    Lifting through all the
    Gently-breasted
    Counties of England.

When the swallow snips the string that holds the world in
  And the ring-dove claps and nearly loops the loop
You just can't count everything that follows in a tumble
  Like a whole circus tumbling through a hoop

    Grass in a mesh of all flowers floundering
    Sizzling leaves and blossoms bombing
    Nestlings hissing and groggy-legged insects

                    And the trees
    Stagger, they stronger

Brace their boles and biceps under
The load of gift. And the hills float
Light as bubble glass
On the smoke-blue evening

And rabbits are bobbing everywhere, and a thrush
Rings coolly in a far corner. A shiver of green
Strokes the darkening slope as the land
Begins her labour.

TED HUGHES

Pilgrimage

Whan that Aprille with his shoures sote
The droghte of Marche hath perced to the rote,
And bathed every veyne in switch licour,
Of which vertu engendred is the flour;
Whan Zephirus eek with his swete breeth
Inspired hath in every holt and heeth
The tendre croppes, and the yonge sonne
Hath in the Ram his halfe cours y-ronne,
And smale fowles maken melodye,
That slepen all the night with open yë,
(So priketh hem nature in hir corages*):
Than longen folk to goon on pilgrimages
(And palmers for to seken straunge strondes)
To ferne halwes†, couthe in sondry londes;
And specially, from every shires ende
Of Engelond, to Caunterbury they wende,

* hearts   † distant shrines

28

The holy blisful martir for to seke,
That hem hath holpen, whan that they were seke. . . .

GEOFFREY CHAUCER
from the Prologue to *The Canterbury Tales*

Cuccu Song

Sumer is icumen in;
   Lhude sing cuccu!
Groweth sed, and bloweth med,
   And springeth the wude nu.
     Sing cuccu!

Awe bleteth after lomb,
   Lhouth after calve cu;
Bulluc sterteth, bucke verteth,
   Murie sing cuccu!

Cuccu, cuccu, well singes thu, cuccu:
Ne swike* thu naver nu:
Sing cuccu, nu, sing cuccu,
   Sing cuccu, sing cuccu, nu!

ANON.
England, thirteenth century

* cease

Adlestrop

Yes. I remember Adlestrop—
The name, because one afternoon
Of heat the express-train drew up there
Unwontedly. It was late June.

The steam hissed. Someone cleared his throat.
No one left and no one came
On the bare platform. What I saw
Was Adlestrop—only the name

And willows, willow-herb, and grass,
And meadowsweet, and haycocks dry,
No whit less still and lonely fair
Than the high cloudlets in the sky.

And for that minute a blackbird sang
Close by, and round him, mistier,
Farther and farther, all the birds
Of Oxfordshire and Gloucestershire.

EDWARD THOMAS

When the Cows Come Home

When the cows come home the milk is coming;
Honey's made while the bees are humming;
Duck and drake on the rushy lake,
And the deer live safe in the breezy brake;
And timid, funny, pert little bunny
Winks his nose, and sits all sunny.

CHRISTINA ROSSETTI

Mr. Bidery's Spidery Garden

Poor old Mr. Bidery.
His garden's awfully spidery:
Bugs use it as a hidery.

In April it was seedery,
By May a mass of weedery;
And oh, the bugs! How greedery.

White flowers out or buddery,
Potatoes made it spuddery;
And when it rained, what muddery!

June days grow long and shaddery;
Bullfrog forgets his taddery;
The spider legs his laddery.

With cabbages so odory,
Snapdragon soon explodery,
At twilight all is toadery.

Young corn still far from foddery
No sign of goldenrodery,
Yet feeling low and doddery

Is poor old Mr. Bidery,
His garden lush and spidery,
His apples green, not cidery.

Pea-picking *is* so poddery!

DAVID MCCORD

Autumn

Yellow the bracken,
  Golden the sheaves,
Rosy the apples,
  Crimson the leaves;
Mist on the hillside,
  Clouds grey and white,
Autumn, good morning,
  Summer, good night!

FLORENCE HOATSON

Sweet Chestnuts

How still the woods were! Not a redbreast whistled
To mark the end of a mild autumn day.
Under the trees the chestnut-cases lay,
Looking like small green hedgehogs softly bristled.

Plumply they lay, each with its fruit packed tight;
For when we rolled them gently with our feet,
The outer shells burst wide apart and split,
Showing the chestnuts brown and creamy-white.

Quickly we kindled a bright fire of wood,
And placed them in the ashes. There we sat,
Listening how all our chestnuts popped and spat.
And then, the smell how rich, the taste how good!

JOHN WALSH

The Autumn Robin

Sweet little bird in russet coat,
 The livery of the closing year,
I love thy lonely plaintive note
 And tiny whispering song to hear.
While on the stile or garden seat
 I sit to watch the falling leaves,
The song thy little joys repeat
 My loneliness relieves.

JOHN CLARE
from *The Autumn Robin*

Reality Breaks In

Chips

Out of the paper bag
Comes the hot breath of the chips
And I shall blow on them
To stop them burning my lips.

Before I leave the counter
The woman shakes
Raindrops of vinegar on them
And salty snowflakes.

Outside the frosty pavements
Are slippery as a slide
But the chips and I
Are warm inside.

STANLEY COOK

If You Don't Put Your Shoes On

If you don't put your shoes on before I count fifteen then
we won't go to the woods to climb the chestnut, one
   But I can't find them.
Two.
   I can't
They're under the sofa, three
   No. O yes
Four five six
   Stop—they've got knots they've got knots
You should untie the laces when you take your shoes off, seven
   Will you do one shoe while I do the other then?
Eight, but that would be cheating
   Please
Alright
   It always . . .
Nine
   It always sticks—I'll use my teeth
Ten
   It won't it won't. It has—look
Eleven
   I'm not wearing any socks.
Twelve
   Stop counting stop counting. Mum, where are my socks,
      mum?
They're in your shoes. Where you left them.
   I didn't.
Thirteen
   O they're inside out and upside down and bundled up
Fourteen
   Have you done the knot on the shoe you were . . .

Yes, put it on the right foot
  But socks don't have a right and wrong foot
The shoes silly. Fourteen and a half.
  I am I am. Wait
  Don't go to the woods without me
  Look that's one shoe already
Fourteen and three quarters
  There
You haven't tied the bows yet
  We could do them on the way there
No we won't. Fourteen and seven eighths
  Help me then.
  You know I'm not fast at bows
Fourteen and fifteen sixteeenths
  A single bow is alright isn't it?
Fifteen. We're off.
  See I did it.
  Didn't I?

MICHAEL ROSEN

Birds in the Garden

Greedy little sparrow,
  Great big crow,
Saucy little tom-tits
  All in a row.

Are you very hungry,
  No place to go?
Come and eat my breadcrumbs,
  In the snow.

ANON.

Child on Top of a Greenhouse

The wind billowing out the seat of my britches,
My feet crackling splinters of glass and dried putty,
The half grown chrysanthemums staring up like accusers,
Up through the streaked glass, flashing with sunlight,
A few white clouds all rushing eastward,
A line of elms plunging and tossing like horses,
And everyone, everyone pointing up and shouting!

THEODORE ROETHKE

Five Eyes

In Hans' old Mill his three black cats
Watch his bins for the thieving rats.
Whisker and claw, they crouch in the night,
Their five eyes smouldering green and bright:
Squeaks from the flour sacks, squeaks from where
The cold wind stirs on the empty stair,
Squeaking and scampering, everywhere.
Then down they pounce, now in, now out,
At whisking tail, and sniffing snout;
While lean old Hans he snores away
Till peep of light at break of day;
Then up he climbs to his creaking mill,
Out come his cats all grey with meal—
Jekkel, and Jessup, and one-eyed Jill.

WALTER DE LA MARE

Glass Falling

The glass is going down. The sun
Is going down. The forecasts say
It will be warm, with frequent showers.
We ramble down the showery hours
And amble up and down the day.
Mary will wear her black goloshes
And splash the puddles on the town;
And soon on fleets of macintoshes
The rain is coming down, the frown
Is coming down of heaven showing
A wet night coming, the glass is going
Down, the sun is going down.

LOUIS MACNEICE

Noise

Billy is blowing his trumpet;
Bertie is banging a tin;
Betty is crying for Mummy
And Bob has pricked Ben with a pin.
Baby is crying out loudly;
He's out on the lawn in his pram.
I am the only one silent
And I've eaten all of the jam.

ANON.

Advice to Children and their Parents

Children attend!
You had better not be born than not be taught:
  and you must not always have your own way.

Tell the truth, and don't be obstinate and
  rebellious.

Hold up your head,
Wash your face and hands,
Be always courteous.

Don't throw stones at dogs nor hogs,
Nor at men's windows.

Don't go birds nesting,
Don't go out to steal fruit.

Don't make faces at any man.

Eat what's given you,
And may God keep you good.

ANON.

Arranged from F. J. Furnivall's annotated edition of
The Babees Book of 1475

Animals and Friends

Nicholas Nye

Thistle and darnel and dock grew there,
 And a bush, in a corner, of may;
On the orchard wall I used to sprawl
 In the blazing heat of the day;
Half asleep and half awake,
 While the birds went twittering by,
And nobody there my lone to share
 But Nicholas Nye.

Nicholas Nye was lean and grey,
 Lame of a leg and old,
More than a score of donkey's years
 He had seen since he was foaled;
He munched the thistles, purple and spiked,
 Would sometimes stop and sigh,
And turn his head, as if he said,
 "Poor Nicholas Nye!"

Alone with his shadow he'd drowse in the meadow,
 Lazily swinging his tail;
At break of day he used to bray,—
 Not much too hearty and hale.
But a wonderful gumption was under his skin,
 And a clear calm light in his eye,
And once in a while he would smile a smile
 Would Nicholas Nye.

Seem to be smiling at me, he would,
From his bush, in the corner, of may—

Bony and ownerless, widowed and worn,
    Knobble-kneed, lonely and grey;
And over the grass would seem to pass
    'Neath the deep dark blue of the sky,
Something much better than words between me
    And Nicholas Nye.

But dusk would come in the apple boughs,
    The green of the glow-worm shine,
The birds in nest would crouch to rest,
And home I'd trudge to mine;
And there, in the moonlight, dark with dew,
    Asking not wherefore nor why,
Would brood like a ghost, and as still as a post,
    Old Nicholas Nye.

WALTER DE LA MARE

The Prayer of the Little Ducks

Dear God,
give us a flood of water.
Let it rain tomorrow and always.
Give us plenty of little slugs
and other luscious things to eat.
Protect all folk who quack
and everyone who knows how to swim.
Amen.

CARMEN BERNOS DE GASZTOLD
translated by Rumer Godden

Reynard

Round Miss Bell's pond the grasses and weeds
Grow thick and tall with brambles and reeds
When Autumn leaves fall;
A brownish-tawny,
Yellowish-fawny
Tangle to hide in,
A fox-coloured place
With water to slide in
For Reynard, gone lame,
With hounds behind him.
. . . So that's where he came.

"I bet they don't find him!"

Said wrinkled Miss Bell.
She didn't tell
Though, from the window, she saw the reeds quiver,
Saw Reynard, tongue-lolling, start, wince and shiver
Into the shadowed pond and lie
Nose up, stone still, till hounds had passed by.

Now hounds are fed, the village sleeping;
Muddied, smiling, Reynard's creeping
Past the moonlit hips and haws
. . . Miss Bell's hen clamped in his jaws.

GWEN DUNN

Cows

Half the time they munched the grass, and all the time
   they lay
Down in the water-meadows, the lazy month of May,
      A-chewing,
      A-mooing,
    To pass the hours away.

   "Nice weather," said the brown cow.
    "Ah," said the white.
  "Grass is very tasty."
   "Grass is all right."

Half the time they munched the grass, and all the time
   they lay
Down in the water-meadows, the lazy month of May,

> A-chewing,
> A-mooing,
> To pass the hours away.

> "Rain coming," said the brown cow.
> "Ah," said the white.
> "Flies is very tiresome."
> "Flies bite."

Half the time they munched the grass, and all the time
  they lay
Down in the water-meadows, the lazy month of May,
> A-chewing,
> A-mooing,
> To pass the hours away.

> "Time to go," said the brown cow.
> "Ah," said the white.
> "Nice chat." "Very pleasant."
> "Night." "Night."

Half the time they munched the grass, and all the time
  they lay
Down in the water-meadows, the lazy month of May,
> A-chewing,
> A-mooing,
> To pass the hours away.

JAMES REEVES

Lone Dog

I'm a lean dog, a keen dog, a wild dog, and lone;
I'm a rough dog, a tough dog, hunting on my own;
I'm a bad dog, a mad dog, teasing silly sheep;
I love to sit and bay the moon, to keep fat souls from sleep.

I'll never be a lap dog, licking dirty feet,
A sleek dog, a meek dog, cringing for my meat;
Not for me the fireside, the well-filled plate,
But shut door, and sharp stone, and cuff, and kick, and hate.

Not for me the other dogs, running by my side;
Some have run a short while, but none of them would bide.
O mine is still the lone trail, the hard trail, the best,
Wide wind, and wild stars, and the hunger of the quest!

IRENE MCLEOD

Dogs

I had a little dog,
    and my dog was very small.
He licked me in the face,
    and he answered to my call.
Of all the treasures that were mine,
    I loved him best of all.

FRANCES CORNFORD

The Cat of Cats

I am the cat of cats. I am
   The everlasting cat!
Cunning, and old, and sleek as jam,
   The everlasting cat!
I hunt the vermin in the night—
   The everlasting cat!
For I see best without the light—
   The everlasting cat!

WILLIAM BRIGHTY RANDS

Young Lambs

The spring is coming by a many signs;
The trays are up, the hedges broken down
That fenced the haystack, and the remnant shines
Like some old antique fragment weathered brown.
And where suns peep, in every sheltered place,
The little early buttercups unfold
A glittering star or two—till many trace
The edges of the blackthorn clumps in gold.
And then a little lamb bolts up behind
The hill, and wags his tail to meet the yoe;*
And then another, sheltered from the wind,
Lies all his length as dead—and lets me go
Close by, and never stirs, but basking lies,
With legs stretched out as though he could not rise.

JOHN CLARE

* ewe

53

The Three Little Pigs

A jolly old sow once lived in a sty,
   And three little piggies had she,
And she waddled about saying "Umph! umph! umph!"
   While the little ones said "Wee! wee!"
"My dear little brothers," said one of the brats,
   "My dear little piggies," said he;
"Let us all for the future say Umph! umph! umph!
   "'Tis so childish to say Wee! wee!"

Then these little pigs grew skinny and lean,
   And lean they might very well be;
For somehow they *couldn't* say "Umph! umph! umph!"
   And they *wouldn't* say "Wee! wee! wee!"

So after a time these little pigs died,
   They all died of *felo de se**;
From trying too hard to say "Uumph! umph! umph!"
   When they only could say "Wee! wee!"

Moral

A moral there is to this little song,
   A moral that's easy to see;
Don't try when you're young to say "Umph! umph! umph!"
   For you only can say "Wee! wee!"

ALFRED SCOTT GATTY

* *felo de se*, suicide

55

Hunter Trials

It's awf'lly bad luck on Diana,
   Her ponies have swallowed their bits;
She fished down their throats with a spanner
   And frightened them all into fits.

So now she's attempting to borrow.
   Do lend her some bits, Mummy, do;
I'll lend her my own for tomorrow,
   But today, I'll be wanting them too.

Just look at Prunella on Guzzle,
   The wizardest pony on earth;
Why doesn't she slacken the muzzle
   And tighten the breech in his girth?

I say, Mummy, there's Mrs. Geyser
   And doesn't she look pretty sick?
I bet it's because Mona Lisa
   Was hit on the hock with a brick.

Miss Blewitt says Monica threw it,
   But Monica says it was Joan
And Joan's very thick with Miss Blewitt,
   So Monica's sulking alone.

And Margaret failed in her paces,
   Her withers got tied in a noose,
So her coronets caught in the traces
   And now all her fetlocks are loose.

Oh, it's me now. I'm terribly nervous.
   I wonder if Smudges will shy.
She's practically certain to swerve as
   Her Pelham is over one eye.

.   .   .

Oh wasn't it naughty of Smudges?
   Oh, Mummy, I'm sick with disgust,
She threw me in front of the Judges,
   And my silly old collarbone's bust.

JOHN BETJEMAN

Who's In?

"The door is shut fast
   And everyone's out."
But people don't know
   What they're talking about!
Say the fly on the wall,
And the flame on the coals,
And the dog on his rug,
And the mice in their holes,
And the kitten curled up,
And the spiders that spin—
"What, everyone out?
Why, everyone's in!"

ELIZABETH FLEMING

The Mare

Look at the mare of Farmer Giles!
She's brushing her hooves on the mat;

Look at the mare of Farmer Giles!
She's knocked on the door, rat-a-tat!

With a clack of her hoof and a wave of her head
She's tucked herself up in the four-post bed,
    And she's wearing the Farmer's hat!

HERBERT ASQUITH

My Brother Bert

Pets are the Hobby of my brother Bert.
He used to go to school with a Mouse in his shirt.

His Hobby it grew, as some hobbies will,
And grew and GREW and GREW until—

Oh don't breathe a word, pretend you haven't heard.
A simply appalling thing has occurred—

The very thought makes me iller and iller:
Bert's brought home a gigantic Gorilla!

If you think that's really not such a scare,
What if it quarrels with his Grizzly Bear?

You still think you could keep your head?
What if the Lion from under the bed

And the four Ostriches that deposit
Their football eggs in his bedroom closet

And the Aardvark out of his bottom drawer
All danced out and joined in the Roar?

What if the Pangolins were to caper
Out of their nests behind the wallpaper?

With the fifty sorts of Bats
That hang on his hatstand like old hats,

And out of a shoebox the excitable Platypus
Along with the Ocelot or Jungle-Cattypus?

The Wombat, the Dingo, the Gecko, the Grampus—
How they would shake the house with their Rumpus!

Not to forget the Bandicoot
Who would certainly peer from his battered old boot.

Why it would be a dreadful day,
And what Oh what would the neighbours say!

TED HUGHES

The Family

Widdy-widdy-wurkey
Is the name of my turkey;
There-and-back-again
Is the name of my hen;
Waggle-tail-loose
Is the name of my goose;
Widdy-widdy-wurkey
Is the name of my turkey.

Widdy-widdy-wurkey
Is the name of my turkey;
Quackery-quack
Is the name of my duck;
Grummelty-grig
Is the name of my pig;
Widdy-widdy-wurkey
Is the name of my turkey.

Widdy-widdy-wurkey
Is the name of my turkey;
Tinker-Tog
Is the name of my dog;

Velvety-pat
Is the name of my cat;
Widdy-widdy-wurkey
Is the name of my turkey.

Widdy-widdy-wurkey
Is the name of my turkey;
Fiery-speed
Is the name of my steed;
Run-of-the-house
Is the name of my mouse;
Widdy-widdy-wurkey
Is the name of my turkey.

Widdy-widdy-wurkey
Is the name of my turkey;
Very-well-done
Is the name of my son;
Dearer-than-life
Is the name of my wife;
Widdy-widdy-wurkey
Is the name of my turkey.

And now you know my famil*ee*
And all that does belong to me.

ROSE FYLEMAN

61

The Song of Quoodle

They haven't got no noses,
The fallen sons of Eve;
Even the smell of roses
Is not what they supposes;
But more than mind discloses
And more than men believe.

The brilliant smell of water,
The brave smell of a stone,
The smell of dew and thunder,
The old bones buried under,
Are things in which they blunder
And err, if left alone.

The wind from winter forests,
The scent of scentless flowers,
The breath of brides' adorning,
The smell of snare and warning,
The smell of Sunday morning,
God gave to us for ours.

*　　　*　　　*

And Quoodle here discloses
All things that Quoodle can,
They haven't got no noses,
They haven't got no noses,

And goodness only knowses
The Noselessness of Man.

G. K. CHESTERTON

Jim-Jam Pyjamas

He wears striped jim-jam pyjamas,
You never saw jim-jams like those,
A fine-fitting, stretchy, fur cat-suit,
Skin-tight from his head to his toes.

He wears striped jim-jam pyjamas,
Black and yellow and dashingly gay;
He makes certain that everyone sees them
By keeping them on all the day.

He wears striped jim-jam pyjamas,
He walks with a smug-pussy stride;
There's no hiding his pride in his jim-jams
With their zig-zaggy lines down each side.

He wears striped jim-jam pyjamas
And pauses at times to display
The effect as he flexes his torso—
Then he fancies he hears people say:

"I wish I had jim-jam pyjamas!
I wish I were feline and slim!
Oh, look at that brave Bengal tiger!
Oh, how I should love to be him!"

GINA WILSON

A Knight

A Knight ther was, and that a worthy man
That fro the tyme that he first bigan
To ryden out, he loved chivalrye,
Trouthe and honour, fredom and curteisye.
Ful worthy was he in his lordes werre,
And therto hadde he riden (no man ferre*)
As well in Cristendom as hethenesse,
And ever honoured for his worthinesse. . . .
At mortal batailles hadde he been fiftene,
And foughten for our feith at Tramissene
In listes thryes, and ay slayn his fo.
This like worthy knight had been also
Somtyme with the lord of Palatye, ·
Ageyn another hethen in Turkye:
And evermore he hadde a sovereyn prys.
And though that he were worthy, he was wys,
And of his port† as meke as is a mayde.
He never yet no vileinye ne sayde
In all his lyf, un-to no maner wight.
He was a verray parfit gentil knight.

GEOFFREY CHAUCER
from the Prologue to *The Canterbury Tales*

* further   † behaviour

A Squire

With him ther was his sone, a yong Squyer,
A lovyere, and a lusty bacheler,
With lokkes crulle*, as they were leyd in presse.
Of twenty yeer of age he was, I gesse.
Of his stature he was of evene lengthe,
And wonderly deliver†, and greet of strengthe.
And he had been somtyme in chivachye,
In Flaundres, in Artoys, and Picardye,
And born him wel, as of so litel space,
In hope to stonden in his lady grace.
Embrouded was he, as it were a mede
Al ful of fresshe floures, whyte and rede.
Singinge he was, or floytinge‡, all the day;
He was as fresh as is the month of May.
Short was his goune, with sleves longe and wyde.
Wel coude he sitte on hors, and faire ryde.
He coude songes make and wel endyte§,
Juste and eek daunce, and wel purtreye and wryte.
So hote he lovede, that by nightertale
He sleep namore than dooth a nightingale.
Curteys he was, lowly, and servisable,
And carf biforn his fader at the table.

GEOFFREY CHAUCER
from the Prologue to *The Canterbury Tales*

* curled   † agile
‡ playing the flute   § write down

Fantastical

The Fairies

When mortals are at rest,
And snoring in their nest;
Unheard and unespied,
Through keyholes we do glide;
Over tables, stools and shelves,
We trip it with our fairy elves.

And if the house be foul
With platter, dish or bowl,
Upstairs we nimbly creep,
And find the sluts asleep:
There we pinch their arms and thighs:
None escapes, nor none espies.

But if the house be swept,
And from uncleanness kept,
We praise the household maid,
And duly she is paid:
For we use before we go
To drop a tester* in her shoe.

ANON.

from *The Fairy Queen*

* sixpence

Two Limericks

There was an old Person of Sparta,
Who had twenty-five sons and one daughter;
He fed them on snails
And weighed them in scales,
That wonderful Person of Sparta.

There was a young lady of Niger,
Who smiled as she rode on a tiger;
They came back from the ride,
With the lady inside,
And a smile on the face of the tiger.

EDWARD LEAR

Jabberwocky

'Twas brillig, and the slithy toves
 Did gyre and gimble in the wabe:
All mimsy were the borogoves,
  And the mome raths outgrabe.

"Beware the Jabberwock, my son!
 The jaws that bite, the claws that catch!
Beware the Jubjub bird, and shun
 The frumious Bandersnatch!"

He took his vorpal sword in hand:
 Long time the manxome foe he sought—
So rested he by the Tumtum tree,
 And stood awhile in thought.

And, as in uffish thought he stood,
 The Jabberwock, with eyes of flame,
Came whiffling through the tulgey wood,
 And burbled as it came!

One, two! One, two! And through and through
 The vorpal blade went snicker-snack!
He left it dead, and with its head
 He went galumphing back.

"And hast thou slain the Jabberwock?
 Come to my arms, my beamish boy!
O frabjous day! Callooh! Callay!"
 He chortled in his joy.

'Twas brillig, and the slithy toves
  Did gyre and gimble in the wabe:
All mimsy were the borogoves,
  And the mome raths outgrabe.

LEWIS CARROLL
from *Through the Looking-Glass*

The Marrog

My desk's at the back of the class
  And nobody, nobody knows
    I'm a Marrog from Mars
With a body of brass
  And seventeen fingers and toes.

Wouldn't they shriek if they knew
  I've three eyes at the back of my head
And my hair is bright purple
My nose is deep blue
  And my teeth are half-yellow, half-red

My five arms are silver, and spiked
  With knives on them sharper than spears.
I could go back right now, if I liked—
  And return in a million light-years.

I could gobble them all,
For I'm seven foot tall
And I'm breathing green flames from my ears.

Wouldn't they yell if they knew,
  If they guessed that a Marrog was here?
Ha–ha, they haven't a clue—
  Or wouldn't they tremble with fear!
"Look, look, a Marrog"
  They'd all scream—and SMACK
The blackboard would fall and the ceiling would crack
  And teacher would faint, I suppose.
But I grin to myself, sitting right at the back
  And nobody, nobody knows.

R. C. SCRIVEN

Tom Thumb's Epitaph

Here lies Tom Thumb, King Arthur's Knight,
Who died by a spider's cruel bite.
He was well known in Arthur's court,
Where he afforded gallant sport.
He rode at tilt and tournament,
And on a mouse a-hunting went.
Alive he filled the court with mirth;
His death to sorrow soon gave birth.
Wipe, wipe your eyes and shake your head
And cry,—Alas! Tom Thumb is dead.

ANON.

A Finger of Fear

Fairy Story

I went into the wood one day
And there I walked and lost my way

When it was so dark I could not see
A little creature came to me

He said if I would sing a song
The time would not be very long

But first I must let him hold my hand tight
Or else the wood would give me a fright

I sang a song, he let me go
But now I am home again there is nobody I know.

STEVIE SMITH

What Has Happened to Lulu?

What has happened to Lulu, Mother?
    What has happened to Lu?
There's nothing in her bed but an old rag-doll
    And by its side a shoe.

Why is her window wide, Mother,
    The curtain flapping free,
And only a circle on the dusty shelf
    Where her money-box used to be?

Why do you turn your head, Mother,
   And why do the tear-drops fall?
And why do you crumple that note on the fire
   And say it is nothing at all?

I woke to voices late last night,
   I heard an engine roar.
Why do you tell me the things I heard
   Were a dream and nothing more?

I heard somebody cry, Mother,
   In anger or in pain,
But now I ask you why, Mother,
   You say it was a gust of rain.

Why do you wander about as though
   You don't know what to do?
What has happened to Lulu, Mother?
   What has happened to Lu?

CHARLES CAUSLEY

Now the Hungry Lion Roars

Now the hungry lion roars,
   And the wolf behowls the moon;
Whilst the heavy ploughman snores,
   All with weary task fordone.
Now the wasted brands do glow,
   Whilst the screech-owl, screeching loud,
Puts the wretch that lies in woe
   In remembrance of a shroud.

Now it is the time of night
   That the graves, all gaping wide,
Every one lets forth his sprite,
   In the churchway paths to glide:
And we fairies, that do run
   By the triple Hecate's team,
From the presence of the sun,
   Following darkness like a dream,
Now are frolic; not a mouse
Shall disturb this hallowed house;
I am sent with broom before,
To sweep the dust behind the door.

Through the house give glimmering light,
   By the dead and drowsy fire;
Every elf and fairy sprite
   Hop as light as bird from brier;
And this ditty, after me,
Sing, and dance it, trippingly.
First rehearse your song by rote,
To each word a warbling note:
Hand in hand, with fairy grace,
Will we sing, and bless this place.

WILLIAM SHAKESPEARE
from *A Midsummer Night's Dream*

The Serpent

There was a Serpent who had to sing.
There was. There was.
He simply gave up Serpenting.
Because. Because.

He didn't like his Kind of Life;
He couldn't find a proper Wife;
He was a Serpent with a soul;
He got no Pleasure down his Hole.
And so, of course, he had to Sing,
And Sing he did, like Anything!
The Birds, they were, they were Astounded;
And various Measures Propounded
To stop the Serpent's Awful Racket:
They bought a Drum. He wouldn't Whack it.
They sent,—you always send,—to Cuba
And got a Most Commodious Tuba;
They got a Horn, they got a Flute,
But Nothing would suit.
He said, "Look, Birds, all this is futile:
I do *not* like to Bang or Tootle."
And then he cut loose with a Horrible Note
That practically split the Top of his Throat.
"You see," he said, with a Serpent's Leer,
"I'm Serious about my Singing Career!"
And the Woods Resounded with many a Shriek
As the Birds flew off to the End of Next Week.

THEODORE ROETHKE

Hide and Seek

Call out. Call loud: "I'm ready! Come and find me!"
The sacks in the toolshed smell like the seaside.
They'll never find you in this salty dark,
But be careful that your feet aren't sticking out.
Wiser not to risk another shout.
The floor is cold. They'll probably be searching
The bushes near the swing. Whatever happens
You mustn't sneeze when they come prowling in.
And here they are, whispering at the door;
You've never heard them sound so hushed before.
Don't breathe. Don't move. Stay dumb. Hide in your
  blindness.
They're moving closer, someone stumbles, mutters;
Their words and laughter scuffle, and they're gone.
But don't come out just yet; they'll try the lane
And then the greenhouse and back here again.
They must be thinking that you're very clever,
Getting more puzzled as they search all over.
It seems a long time since they went away.
Your legs are stiff, the cold bites through your coat;
The dark damp smell of sand moves in your throat.
It's time to let them know that you're the winner.
Push off the sacks. Uncurl and stretch. That's better!
Out of the shed and call to them: "I've won!
Here I am! Come and own up I've caught you!"
The darkening garden watches. Nothing stirs.
The bushes hold their breath; the sun is gone.
Yes, here you are. But where are they who sought you?

VERNON SCANNELL

The Wind Was on the Withered Heath

The wind was on the withered heath,
but in the forest stirred no leaf:
there shadows lay by night and day,
and dark things silent crept beneath.

The wind came down from mountains cold,
and like a tide it roared and rolled;
the branches groaned, the forest moaned,
and leaves were laid upon the mould.

The wind went on from West to East;
all movement in the forest ceased,
but shrill and harsh across the marsh
its whistling voices were released.

The grasses hissed, their tassels bent,
the reeds were rattling—on it went.
o'er shaken pool under heavens cool
where racing clouds were torn and rent.

It passed the lonely Mountain bare
and swept above the dragon's lair:
there black and dark lay boulders stark
and flying smoke was in the air.

It left the world and took its flight
over the wide seas of the night.
The moon set sail upon the gale,
and stars were fanned to leaping light.

J. R. R. TOLKIEN
from *The Hobbit*

The Knight of the Grail

Lully, lulley; lully, lulley;
The fawcon hath born my mak* away.

He bare hym vp, he bare hym down;
He bare hym into an orchard brown.

In that orchard ther was an hall,
That was hangid with purpill and pall.

And in that hall ther was a bede;
Hit was hangid with gold so rede.

And yn that bed ther lythe a knyght,
His wowndes bledyng day and nyght.

By that bedes side ther kneleth a may,
And she wepeth both nyght and day.

And by that beddes side ther stondith a ston,
"Corpus Christi" wretyn theron.

ANON.
(*Sixteenth century*)

* mate

Steam Shovel

The dinosaurs are not all dead.
I saw one raise its iron head
To watch me walking down the road
Beyond our house today.
Its jaws were dripping with a load
Of earth and grass that it had cropped,
It must have heard me where I stopped,
Snorted white steam my way,
And stretched its long neck out to see,
And chewed, and grinned quite amiably.

CHARLES MALAM

A Small Dragon

I've found a small dragon in the woodshed.
Think it must have come from deep inside a forest
because it's damp and green and leaves
are still reflecting in its eyes.

I fed it on many things, tried grass,
the roots of stars, hazel-nut and dandelion,
but it stared up at me as if to say, I need
foods you can't provide.

It made a nest among the coal,
not unlike a bird's but larger,
it is out of place here
and is quite silent.

If you believed in it I would come
hurrying to your house to let you share my wonder,
but I want instead to see
if you yourself will pass this way.

Spinning Song

The miller's daughter
Combs her hair,
Like flocks of doves
As soft as vair . . .

Oh, how those soft flocks flutter down
Over the empty grassy town.

Like a queen in a crown
Of gold light, she
Sits 'neath the shadows'
Flickering tree—

Till the old dame went the way she came,
Playing bob-cherry with a candle-flame.

Now Min the cat
With her white velvet gloves
Watches where sat
The mouse with her loves—

(Old and malicious Mrs. Grundy
Whose washing-day is from Monday to Monday).

"Not a crumb," said Min,
"To a mouse I'll be giving,
For a mouse must spin
To earn her living."

So poor Mrs. Mouse and her three cross Aunts
Nibble snow that rustles like gold wheat plants.

And the miller's daughter
Combs her locks,
Like running water
Those dove-soft flocks;

And her mouth is sweet as a honey-flower cold
But her heart is heavy as bags of gold.

The shadow-mice said,
"We will line with down
From those doves, our bed
And our slippers and gown,

For everything comes to the shadows at last
If the spinning-wheel Time move slow or fast."

EDITH SITWELL

Old Songs to Sing:
Old Tales to Tell

Casey Jones

Come all you rounders if you want to hear
A story all about a brave engineer.
Casey Jones was the rounder's name,
On a six-eight wheeler, boys, he won his fame.

The caller called Casey at a half-past four;
Kissed his wife at the station door;
Mounted to the cabin with his orders in his hand,
And took his farewell trip to that promised land.

   Casey Jones! Mounted to the cabin,
   Casey Jones! With his orders in his hand,
   Casey Jones! Mounted to the cabin
   And took his farewell trip to that promised land.

Put in your water and shovel in your coal;
Put your head out the window, watch them drivers roll.
I'll run her till she leaves the rail,
'Cause I'm eight hours late with that western mail.

He looked at his watch and his watch was slow;
He looked at the water and the water was low;
He turned to the fireman and then he said,
"We're going to reach Frisco, if we'll all be dead."

   Casey Jones! Going to reach Frisco,
   Casey Jones! If we'll all be dead.
   Casey Jones! Going to reach Frisco.
   We're going to reach Frisco, but we'll all be dead.

Casey pulled up that Reno hill,
He tooted for the crossing; it was awful shrill.
The switchman knew by the engine's moans
That the man at the throttle was Casey Jones.

He pulled up within two miles of the place;
Number Four stared him right in the face;
Turned to the fireman, said, "Boy, you'd better jump;
'Cause there's two locomotives that's going to bump."

    Casey Jones! Two locomotives!
    Casey Jones! That's a-going to bump!
    Casey Jones! Two locomotives!
    There's two locomotives that's a-going to bump.

Casey mumbled just before he died
"There's two more roads that I'd like to ride."
Fireman said, "What can they be?"
"The Southern Pacific and the Santa Fe."

Mrs. Jones sat on her bed a-sighing,
Just received a message that Casey was dying,
Said, "Go to bed, children, and hush your crying,
'Cause you got another papa on the Salt Lake Line.'

    Mrs. Casey Jones! Got another papa!
    Mrs. Casey Jones! On the Salt Lake Line!
    Mrs. Casey Jones! Got another papa!
    And you've got another papa on that Salt Lake Line.

ANON.
(Traditional American)

Didn't It Rain

Now, didn't it rain, chillun,
God's gonna 'stroy this world with water,
Now didn't it rain, my Lord,
Now didn't it rain, rain, rain.

Well, it rained forty days and it rained forty nights,
There wasn't no land nowhere in sight,
God sent a raven to carry the news,
He histe* his wings and away he flew.

Well, it rained forty days and forty nights without stopping,
Noah was glad when the rain stopped a-dropping.
God sent Noah a rainbow sign,
Says, "No more water, but fire next time."

They knocked at the window and they knocked at the door,
They cried, "O Noah, please take me on board."
Noah cried, "You're full of sin,
The Lord's got the key and you can't get in."

ANON.
(Traditional American)

* lifted

It ain't gonna Rain No More, No More

It ain't gonna rain no more, no more,
It ain't gonna rain no more;
How in the heck can I wash my neck
If it ain't gonna rain no more?

ANON.
(Traditional American)

Soldier, Soldier, Won't You Marry Me?

Soldier, soldier, won't you marry me?
  It's O the fife and the drum!
How can I marry such a pretty girl as you
  When I've got no hat to put on!

Off to the tailor's she did go
  As fast as she could run,
Brought him back the finest that was there:
  Now, soldier, put it on!

Soldier, soldier, won't you marry me?
  It's O the fife and the drum!
How can I marry such a pretty girl as you
  When I've got no coat to put on!

Back to the tailor's she did go
  As fast as she could run,
Brought him back the finest that was there:
  Now, soldier, put it on!

Soldier, soldier, won't you marry me?
   It's O the fife and the drum!
How can I marry such a pretty girl as you
   When I've got no shoes to put on!

Off to the shoe-shop she did go
   As fast as she could run,
Brought him back the finest that were there:
   Now, soldier, put them on!

Soldier, soldier, won't you marry me?
   It's O the fife and the drum!
How can I marry such a pretty girl as you
   When I've a wife and babies at home!

ANON.

A Smugglers' Song

If you wake at midnight and hear a horse's feet,
Don't go drawing back the blind, or looking in the street,
Them that asks no questions isn't told a lie.
Watch the wall, my darling, while the Gentlemen go by!
     Five and twenty ponies,
     Trotting through the dark—
     Brandy for the Parson,
     'Baccy for the Clerk;
     Laces for a lady; letters for a spy,
And watch the wall, my darling, while the Gentlemen go by!

Running round the woodlump if you chance to find
Little barrels, roped and tarred, all full of brandy-wine;

Don't you shout to come and look, nor take 'em for your play;
Put the brushwood back again,—and they'll be gone next day!

If you see the stableyard setting open wide;
If you see a tired horse lying down inside;
If your mother mends a coat cut about and tore;
If the lining's wet and warm—don't you ask no more!

If you meet King George's men, dressed in blue and red,
You be careful what you say, and mindful what is said.
If they call you "pretty maid", and chuck you 'neath the chin,
Don't you tell where no one is, nor yet where no one's been!

Knocks and footsteps round the house—whistles after dark—
You've no call for running out till the housedogs bark.
Trusty's here and Pincher's here, and see how dumb they lie—
They don't fret to follow when the Gentlemen go by!

If you do as you've been told, likely there's a chance,
You'll be give a dainty doll, all the way from France,
With a cap of Valenciennes, and a velvet hood—
A present from the Gentlemen, along o' being good!
                    Five and twenty ponies,
                    Trotting through the dark—
                    Brandy for the Parson,
                    'Baccy for the Clerk.
Them that asks no questions isn't told a lie—
Watch the wall, my darling, while the Gentlemen go by!

                                        RUDYARD KIPLING

Get Up and Bar the Door

It fell about the Martinmas time,
    And a gay time it was then,
When our goodwife got puddings to make,
    And she's boiled them in the pan.

The wind so cold blew south and north,
    And blew into the floor;
Quoth our goodman to our goodwife,
    "Get up and bar the door."

"My hand is in my household work,
    Goodman, as ye may see;
And it will not be barred for a hundred years,
    If it's to be barred by me!"

They made a pact between them both,
    They made it firm and sure,
That whosoe'er should speak the first,
    Should rise and bar the door.

Then by there came two gentlemen,
    At twelve o'clock at night,
And they could see neither house nor hall,
    Nor coal nor candlelight.

"Now whether is this a rich man's house,
    Or whether is it a poor?"
But never a word would one of them speak,
    For barring of the door.

The guests they ate the white puddings,
   And then they ate the black;
Tho' much the goodwife thought to herself,
   Yet never a word she spake.

Then said one stranger to the other,
   "Here, man, take ye my knife;
Do ye take off the old man's beard,
   And I'll kiss the goodwife."

"There's no hot water to scrape it off,
   And what shall we do then?"
"Then why not use the pudding broth,
   That boils into the pan?"

O up then started our goodman,
   An angry man was he;
"Will ye kiss my wife before my eyes!
   And with pudding broth scald me!"

Then up and started our goodwife,
   Gave three skips on the floor:
"Goodman, you've spoken the very first word!
   Get up and bar the door!"

ANON.
(English ballad)

The Big Rock Candy Mountains

On a summer's day in the month of May,
A burly bum* come a-hiking,
Travelling down that lonesome road
A-looking for his liking.
He was headed for a land that was far away,
Beside them crystal fountains—
"I'll see you all this coming fall†
In the Big Rock Candy Mountains."

In the Big Rock Candy Mountains
You never change your socks,
And little streams of alcohol
Come a-trickling down the rocks.
The box cars‡ are all empty
And the railroad bulls§ are blind,
There's a lake of stew and whisky, too,
You can paddle all around 'em in a big canoe
In the Big Rock Candy Mountains.

O—the buzzing of the bees in the cigarette trees
Round the soda-water fountains,
Where the lemonade springs and the bluebird sings
In the Big Rock Candy Mountains.

In the Big Rock Candy Mountains,
There's a land that's fair and bright,
Where the hand-outs grow on bushes
And you sleep out every night,
Where the box cars are all empty

* tramp   † autumn   ‡ trucks   § policemen

100

And the sun shines every day,
O I'm bound to go, where there ain't no snow,
Where the rain don't fall and the wind don't blow
In the Big Rock Candy Mountains.

In the Big Rock Candy Mountains
The jails are made of tin
And you can bust right out again
As soon as they put you in;
The farmers' trees are full of fruit,
The barns are full of hay,
I'm going to stay where you sleep all day,
Where they boiled in oil the inventor of toil
In the Big Rock Candy Mountains.

ANON.
(Traditional American)

The Hairy Toe

Once there was a woman went out to pick beans,
and she found a Hairy Toe.
She took the Hairy Toe home with her,
and that night, when she went to bed,
the wind began to moan and groan.
Away off in the distance
she seemed to hear a voice crying,
"Who's got my Hair-r-ry To-o-oe?
Who's got my Hair-r-ry To-o-oe?"

The woman scrooched down,
'way down under the covers,

and about that time
the wind appeared to hit the house,
smoosh,
and the old house creaked and cracked
like something was trying to get in.
The voice had come nearer,
almost at the door now,
and it said,
"Where's my Hair-r-ry To-o-oe?
Who's got my Hair-r-ry To-o-oe?"

The woman scrooched further down
under the covers
and pulled them tight around her head.
The wind growled around the house
like some big animal
and r-r-um-mbled
over the chimbley.
All at once she heard the door cr-r-a-ack
and Something slipped in
and began to creep over the floor.
The floor went
cre-e-eak, cre-e-eak
at every step that thing took towards her bed.
The woman could almost feel
it bending over her bed.
Then in an awful voice it said:
"Where's my Hair-r-ry To-o-oe?
Who's got my Hair-r-ry To-o-oe?
You've got it!"

ANON.
(Traditional American)

The Dragon of Wantley

This dragon had two furious wings
One upon each shoulder,
With a sting in his tail as long as a flail
Which made him bolder and bolder.
He had long claws, and in his jaws
Four and forty teeth of iron,
With a hide as tough as any buff
Which did him round environ.

Have you not heard how the Trojan horse
Held seventy men in his belly?
This dragon wasn't quite so big
But very near I'll tell ye.
Devoured he poor children three
That could not with him grapple,
And at one sup he ate them up
As you would eat an apple.

All sorts of cattle this dragon did eat
Some say he ate up trees,
And that the forests sure he would
Devour by degrees.
For houses and churches were to him
   geese and turkeys
He ate all, and left none behind
But some stones, good sirs, that he
   couldn't crack
Which on the hills you'll find.

ANON.
(from an English folk song)

The Wraggle Taggle Gipsies

There were three gipsies a-come to my door,
And down-stairs ran this a-lady, O!
One sang high, and another sang low,
And the other sang, Bonny, bonny Biscay, O!

Then she pulled off her silk-finished gown
And put on hose of leather, O!
The ragged, ragged rags about our door—
She's gone with the wraggle taggle gipsies, O!

It was late last night, when my lord came home,
Enquiring for his a-lady, O!
The servants said, on every hand:
"She's gone with the wraggle taggle gipsies, O!"

"O saddle to me my milk-white steed,
Go and fetch me my pony, O!
That I may ride and seek my bride,
Who is gone with the wraggle taggle gipsies, O!"

O he rode high and he rode low,
He rode through woods and copses too,
Until he came to an open field,
And there he espied his a-lady, O!

"What makes you leave your house and land?
What makes you leave your money, O?
What makes you leave your new-wedded lord;
To go with the wraggle taggle gipsies, O!"

"What care I for my house and my land?
    What care I for my money, O?
    What care I for my new-wedded lord?
    I'm off with the wraggle taggle gipsies, O!"

"Last night you slept on a goose-feather bed,
    With the sheet turned down so bravely, O!
    And to-night you'll sleep in a cold open field,
    Along with the wraggle taggle gipsies, O!"

"What care I for a goose-feather bed,
    With the sheet turned down so bravely, O?
    For to-night I shall sleep in a cold open field,
    Along with the wraggle taggle gipsies, O!"

ANON.
(English ballad)

Widdecombe Fair

"Tom Pearse, Tom Pearse, lend me your gray mare,"
    All along, down along, out along, lee.
"For I want for to go to Widdecombe Fair,
    Wi' Bill Brewer, Jan Stewer, Peter Gurney, Peter Davy,
    Dan'l Whiddon, Harry Hawk,
  Old Uncle Tom Cobley and all."
        Old Uncle Tom Cobley and all.

"And when shall I see again my gray mare?"
    All along, down along, out along, lee.
"By Friday soon, or Saturday noon,

Wi' Bill Brewer, Jan Stewer, Peter Gurney, Peter Davy,
Dan'l Whiddon, Harry Hawk,
Old Uncle Tom Cobley and all."
Old Uncle Tom Cobley and all.

Then Friday came and Saturday noon,
All along, down along, out along, lee.
But Tom Pearse's old mare hath not trotted home,
Wi' Bill Brewer, Jan Stewer, Peter Gurney, Peter Davy,
Dan'l Whiddon, Harry Hawk,
Old Uncle Tom Cobley and all.
Old Uncle Tom Cobley and all.

So Tom Pearse he got up to the top o' the hill,
All along, down along, out along, lee.
And he seed his old mare down a-making her will,
Wi' Bill Brewer, Jan Stewer, Peter Gurney, Peter Davy,
Dan'll Whiddon, Harry Hawk,
Old Uncle Tom Cobley and all.
Old Uncle Tom Cobley and all.

So Tom Pearse's old mare her took sick and her died,
All along, down along, out along, lee.
And Tom he sat down on a stone, and he cried
Wi' Bill Brewer, Jan Stewer, Peter Gurney, Peter Davy,
Dan'l Whiddon, Harry Hawk,
Old Uncle Tom Cobley and all.
Old Uncle Tom Cobley and all.

But this isn't the end o' this shocking affair,
All along, down along, out along, lee.
Nor, though they be dead, of the horrid career

Of Bill Brewer, Jan Stewer, Peter Gurney, Peter Davy,
  Dan'l Whiddon, Harry Hawk,
Old Uncle Tom Cobley and all.
  Old Uncle Tom Cobley and all.

When the wind whistles cold on the moor of a night,
  All along, down along, out along, lee.
Tom Pearse's old mare doth appear, gashly white,
  Wi' Bill Brewer, Jan Stewer, Peter Gurney, Peter Davy,
  Dan'l Whiddon, Harry Hawk,
Old Uncle Tom Cobley and all.
  Old Uncle Tom Cobley and all.

And all the long night be heard skirling and groans,
  All along, down along, out along, lee.
From Tom Pearse's old mare in her rattling bones,
  And from Bill Brewer, Jan Stewer, Peter Gurney, Peter
  Davy, Dan'l Whiddon, Harry Hawk,
Old Uncle Tom Cobley and all.
  Old Uncle Tom Cobley and all.

ANON.
(Devonshire folksong)

The Land of Story-books

At evening when the lamp is lit,
Around the fire are my parents sit;
They sit at home and talk and sing,
And do not play at anything.

Now, with my little gun I crawl
All in the dark along the wall,

And follow round the forest track
Away behind the sofa back.

There, in the night, where none can spy,
All in my hunter's camp I lie,
And play at books that I have read
Till it is time to go to bed.

These are the hills, these are the woods,
These are my starry solitudes;
And there the river by whose brink
The roaring lions come to drink.

I see the others far away.
As if in firelit camp they lay,
And I, like to an Indian scout,
Around their party prowled about.

So, when my nurse comes in for me,
Home I return across the sea,
And go to bed with backward looks
At my dear land of Story-books.

ROBERT LOUIS STEVENSON

The Lambton Worm

Whisht lads, haud your gobs
I'll tell yes all an awful story
Whisht lads, haud your gobs
I'll tell ye 'boot the worm.

One Sunday morning Lambton went
A-fishing in the Wear
And catched a fish upon his hook
He thowt looked varry queer
But whatna kind of fish it was
Young Lambton couldn't tell
He wouldn't fash to carry it hyem
So he hoyed it doon a well.

Now Lambton felt inclined to gan
And fight in foreign wars
He joined a troop of knights that cared
For neither wounds nor scars
And off he went to Palestine
Where queer things him befell
And varry soon forgot aboot
The queer worm doon the well.

Now this worm got fat and growed and growed
And growed an awful size
Wi' greet big head and greet big gob
And greet big goggly eyes
And when, at neets, he crawled aboot
To pick up bits of news
If he felt dry upon the road
He milked a dozen coos.

This awful worm would often feed
On calves and lambs and sheep
And swellied little bairns alive
When they lay doon to sleep.
And when he'd eaten all he could

And he had had his fill
He crawled away and lapped his tail
Ten times round Penshaw hill.

Now news of this most awful worm
And his queer gannins-on
Soon crossed the seas, got to the ears
Of brave and bold Sir John.
So hyem he come and he catched the beast
And cut it in three halves
And that soon stopped his eating bairns
And sheep and lambs and calves.

Now lads I'll haud me gob
That's all I know aboot the story
Of Sir John's clever job
Wi' the famous Lambton Worm.

ANON.

(Northumberland folk song)

Sir Patrick Spens

The king sits in Dunfermline towne
    Drinking the blood-red wine;
"Oh where will I get a skilful skipper
    To sail this ship of mine?"

Up and spake an elder knight,
    Sat at the king's right knee:
"Sir Patrick Spens is the best sailor
    That ever sailed the sea."

The king has written a broad letter
   And sealed it with his hand.
And sent it to Sir Patrick Spens
   Was walking on the strand.

"To Noroway, to Noroway,
   To Noroway o'er the foam;
The King's own daughter of Noroway,
   'Tis thou must bring her home!"

The first line that Sir Patrick read
   A loud, loud laugh laughed he:
The next line that Sir Patrick read
   The tear blinded his ee.

"Oh who is this has done this deed,
   This ill deed unto me;
To send me out this time o' the year
   To sail upon the sea?

"Make haste, make haste, my merry men all,
   Our good ship sails the morn."
"Oh say not so, my master dear,
   For I fear a deadly storm.

"I saw the new moon late yestere'en
   With the old moon in her arm;
And if we go to sea, master,
   I fear we'll come to harm."

They had not sailed a league, a league,
   A league, but barely three,

When the sky grew dark, the wind blew loud,
  And angry grew the sea.

The anchor broke, the topmast split,
  'Twas such a deadly storm.
The waves came over the broken ship
  Till all her sides were torn.

O long, long may the ladies sit
  With their fans into their hand,
Or ere they see Sir Patrick Spens
  Come sailing to the strand.

O long, long may the maidens stand
  With their gold combs in their hair,
Before they'll see their own dear loves
  Come home to greet them there.

O forty miles off Aberdeen
  'Tis fifty fathom deep.
And there lies good Sir Patrick Spens
  With the Scots lords at his feet.

ANON.
(Scottish ballad)

And Evening Ends

A Fine Day

Clear had the day been from the dawn,
  All chequered was the sky,
Thin clouds, like scarfs of cobweb lawn,
  Veiled heaven's most glorious eye.
The wind had no more strength than this,
  —That leisurely it blew—
To make one leaf the next to kiss
  That closely by it grew.
The rills, that on the pebbles played,
  Might now be heard at will;
This world the only music made,
  Else everything was still.

MICHAEL DRAYTON

The Lightning and Thunder

The lightning and thunder
  They go and they come;
But the stars and the stillness
  Are always at home.

GEORGE MACDONALD

Tumbling

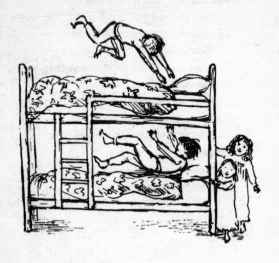

In jumping and tumbling
  We spend the whole day,
Till night by arriving
  Has finished our play.

What then? One and all,
  There's no more to be said,
As we tumbled all day,
  So we tumble to bed.

ANON.

Dream-Pedlary

If there were dreams to sell,
  What would you buy?
Some cost a passing bell;
  Some a light sigh,
That shakes from Life's fresh crown
Only a rose-leaf down.
If there were dreams to sell,
Merry and sad to tell,
And the crier rang the bell,
  What would you buy?
A cottage lone and still,
  With bowers nigh,
Shadowy, my woes to still,
  Until I die.

Such pearl from Life's fresh crown
Fain would I shake me down.
Were dreams to have at will,
This would best heal my ill,
  This would I buy.

THOMAS LOVELL BEDDOES

Aedh Wishes for the Cloths of Heaven

Had I the heavens' embroider'd cloths,
Enwrought with golden and silver light,
The blue and the dim and the dark cloths
Of night and light and the half light,
I would spread the cloths under your feet:
But I, being poor, have only my dreams;
I have spread my dreams under your feet;
Tread softly because you tread on my dreams.

W. B. YEATS

Index of Authors

———•◦◦◦•———

Index of First Lines

THE CLOCK TOWER GHOST

Addlesbury Tower is haunted by Rich King Cole, a mean old man who fell off it long ago in mysterious circumstances. Its newest terror is Mandy – feared by her family and eventually by the ghost too!

NO PLACE LIKE (PUFFIN PLUS)

The day that Pete starts his new college coincides with his determination to be more self-assertive and to prove himself to everybody. He finds himself included in the trendy group at college and suddenly his life is taken over by a succession of discos, parties – and something more sinister in the form of Oliver and Kenny. And then, of course, there was the girl . . .

JASON BODGER AND THE PRIORY GHOST

A ghost story, both funny and exciting, about Jason, the bane of every teacher's life, who is pursued by the ghost of a little nun from the twelfth century!

More Poetry in Puffins

GARGLING WITH JELLY
Brian Patten

A wonderful collection of poems, mostly funny, one or two serious, but all with something to make the reader think twice and perhaps change his or her view of life as a result.

THE WANDERING MOON AND OTHER POEMS
James Reeves

A masterly collection of poems for children, with Edward Ardizzone's illustrations.

NINE O'CLOCK BELL
Raymond Wilson (ed.)

A collection of poems about school for children of 8–12.